I have two Houses

Mummy's house and

Daddy's house

An interactive book

By Shell Hillman

Illustrations by

Kaye Forster

ZEUS

I have Two Houses

Copyright © Shell Hillman 2003

First published by Zeus Publications 2003
http://www.zeus-publications.com
P.O. Box 2554
Burleigh M.D.C.
QLD. 4220
Australia.

ISBN 1 920699 84 8

This book is dedicated to:

Those children who have 2 houses, Mummy's house and Daddy's house.

Dedicated to Georgia & Matthew

I gratefully acknowledge:

Natasha Crow- *Psychologist*
Margaret Maycock- *Diploma of CommunityServices*
(children's services)

Introducing
Michelle (Shell) Hillman

Michelle Hillman known as Shell Hillman is a qualified Social Worker who holds a Bachelor of Social Science, Diploma of Community and Human Service and an Advanced Diploma of Counseling.

Shell has been working with children and families for the past six years. Shell, through her private practice provides counseling to children, youth and families that are affected by separation and divorce, grief and loss and abuse and trauma counseling.

Previously Shell spent three years as a volunteer crisis counselor for the SIDS Foundation, dealing with grief and loss for children and their families. In 1997, Shell founded a youth scholarship scheme called Youth Recovery 2000 for young people between 18-25 years to be trained and gain employment in the hospitality industry.

Currently Shell works for the Abused Child Trust as the Gold Coast Business Development Officer.

As an established author Shell wrote an inspirational book of short stories and poems called Depths of Silence. This book was published on the Gold Coast and proceeds from the book funded Youth Recovery 2000. Shell became well known as an author and public speaker with the book selling 5,000 copies.

Extensive media followed Shell's progress and she was recognised by Larry Anthony (Federal Member for Richmond). Larry Anthony is currently the Minister for Children and Youth Affairs. Shell was invited to a presentation in Canberra in 1997 to address the Department of Education Training and Youth Affairs and received recognition for her continuous work for youth in the Tweed Heads electorate of Richmond.

Shell has a future plan to become an established children's author and advocate for families covering various social issues that affect families today. Shell can also diversify her talents to writing a series of children's interactive books based on the social issue of children going through family divorce.

In society today, statistics indicate that one in every two marriages end in divorce. This has become a social problem that has impacted and placed enormous constraints on our welfare and legal system. Parents need to consider the psychological trauma that children experience when involved in a separation and divorce. A sense of belonging shapes the future existence of children in today's society and the future of our world. This gives us the determination to have desired goals and achieve in a world that is plagued with insecurity and uncertainty.

Assisting children to communicate and understand social issues relating to separation gives parents the opportunity to educate and express their current family unit.

Shell has children of her own and has also experienced the many difficulties as a sole parent. Shell has maintained her career in welfare and has been creating resource material to assist children in counseling. "Is It Me? Mummy and Daddy Breaking Up" and "I have Two Houses" children on access are examples of her work.

Shell has also fundraised for previous charity work with various children's charities.

When Georgia started her new school she had no friends, until she met Matthew.

Georgia walked over to Matthew, who was sitting on the bench in the playground.

"Hello I'm Georgia," she said.

"Hi Georgia, I'm Matthew," he replied.

Use your felt tips or pencils to colour this picture in.

Georgia sat down next to Matthew. They watched the children playing in the schoolyard.

Both Georgia and Matthew started eating their lunch. Matthew noticed that Georgia had a sad look on her face.

Colour this picture in, and then draw some sad faces around the edges of these pages.

"You look sad Georgia," said Matthew.

"Yeah I am sad because I am different to other kids," said Georgia.

Draw a picture of Matthew next to Georgia.

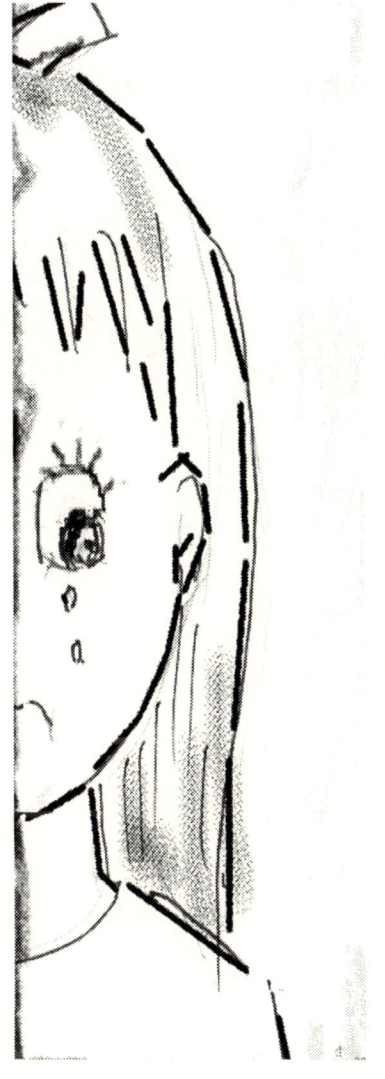

"Why are you different?"
Matthew asked.

Georgia looked at Matthew with her wide blue eyes and replied, "When Mummy and Daddy decided to live in different houses, I didn't know why.

"Mummy and I moved to a different house and Daddy stayed in my other house."

"Mummy said that both she and Daddy still love me, but they had to live in different houses because they were sad.

"So now I have two houses, Mummy's house and Daddy's house," said Georgia.

"I have a Daddy house and a Mummy house too Georgia," squealed Matthew.

He was smiling at Georgia with a look of amazement on his face.

If you have two houses, draw them on these two pages.

"One day I wondered whether Daddy was still my friend because he and Mummy live in different houses. So I asked my Daddy, are you still my friend?"

"Daddy said he is my best friend, even though he and Mummy don't live together anymore."

Draw your Daddy's face in the space above.

19

"Daddy also said he is Mummy's friend too."

Draw your Mummy's face ↑

"Are your Mummy and Daddy still friends Georgia?" Matthew asked.

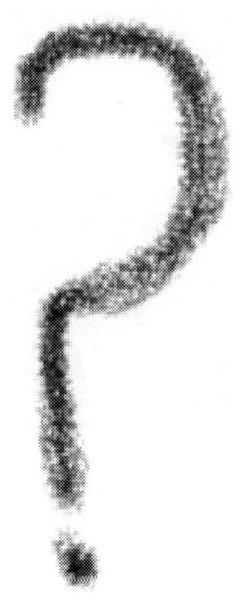

"Yes Matthew, I watch my Mummy and Daddy talk to each other and they both tell me they love me," said Georgia looking at Matthew wide eyed, as she took a bite of her apple.

"Mine too Georgia, would you like one of my biscuits?" Matthew held out his hand.

"No thanks, my Mummy likes me to eat my apple after my sandwich.

"I live with Mummy during the week so I can go to school."

"Mummy picks me up after she finishes work and we go home. I have a bath and she gets dinner ready for me.

"I help Mummy in the kitchen while she is busy cooking. Mummy asks me if I've had a good day at school. I tell her all about my day," said Georgia.

"Who do you live with Matthew?" Georgia moved closer to sit next to Matthew.

"I live with my Daddy some days in the week and on weekends. My daddy also works; he picks me up from our friend's house after work.

"I talk to my Daddy, while he gets my dinner ready. Daddy makes me chicken nuggets, because they are my favorite."

"Daddy and I play together and ride our bikes. Sometimes he takes me to the beach and we walk our dogs.

"I have a special boy's bedroom, with lots of pictures on the wall. I have lots of toys and trucks at my Daddy's house too."

Georgia was so happy she was jumping up and down.

"And I have a special room for me, with dolls and a pram and lots of books to read. Mummy and I have cuddle time and a story before I get ready for bed. When I go to bed at Mummy's house, I take my special teddy with me."

"I sleep in Mummy's bed and in the morning I wake up in my own bed," said Georgia, shaking her head putting her hands on her hips.

"My Daddy does that to me too Georgia. Does your Mummy try to put you to bed early before you're even tired?" Matthew asked.

"Yeah all Daddies and Mummies do that. Just because they are tired; we have to go to bed," said Georgia.

"Yeah, my Daddy just answers the phone and talks to people at work, that's not very tiring."

Draw your Daddy talking on the phone.

"My room is next to Daddy's room. We also have a room at our house for Grandpa Pippy, when he comes to visit. Do you have a room for your Grandpa, Georgia?" Matthew asked.

"No, because my Grandpa and Grandma live next door to my Daddy's house. I see them when I go to Daddy's house," said Georgia.

Grandpa Pippy

Good news page

Senior Citizens

Bad news page

Reporter Joy Love

Kiwis win again

Price rise for senior's hair cuts

rabbits on increase

more bad news

over the page

Girl saves rabbit

"So when do you go to your Daddy's house Georgia?" Matthew asked.

"Every Friday night, my Daddy picks me and my teddy up, and we go to my other house.

"When I am leaving to go to Daddy's, Mummy says, see you soon and have fun. I stay with my Daddy every weekend."

"My Daddy lives on a farm and we have cows. I sit on the back of my Daddy's bike and he takes me on a long ride. I also go for big walks with him."

"Wow Georgia, sounds like you have fun at your Daddy's house," said Matthew.

"When do you go to your Mummy's house Matthew?" Georgia asked.

"I stay at my Mummy's house some days in the week and Mummy and I also have special weekends when my Daddy is working."

"Sometimes when I am at my Mummy's house, I miss my Daddy, so Mummy lets me call him on the telephone and I talk to him; then I feel much better."

"Do you miss your Mummy when you are at your Daddy's house Georgia?" Matthew said.

"Sometimes I do, and I'm always glad to see my Mummy on Monday.

"My cousin Jack doesn't see his Daddy because his Mummy is very angry. My Mummy said that is very sad.

"We are lucky because we are allowed to see and like both our Mummy and Daddy," Georgia said.

"So it is okay to have two houses, a Mummy house and a Daddy house, we are the same Georgia," squealed Matthew.

"Yeah we are and I don't feel sad anymore," said Georgia.

"We will always be friends Georgia because we both have two houses, a Mummy's house and a Daddy's house".

Matthew put his arm around Georgia.

"Yeah and we get to live in both houses," said Georgia.

Draw your best friends on these two pages.

Matthew and Georgia are also lucky that their Mummy and Daddy make sure that they feel safe, by giving them lots of love, talking to them and telling them to have fun when visiting both houses.

The following pages give special tips for Mummies and Daddies.

Tips for Mummies and Daddies

The following tips are a guide to introducing your child to access. It may not always be possible to overcome the emotional reactions that parents and children may have due to their family situation. However they do offer some strategies for parents and children to avoid unnecessary conflict and create quality time with your child. It is important that children have both parents wherever possible.

Try to have a planned activity for you and your child so that at time of pick up to help you and your child bond. Particularly if your access is only a couple of days a week or monthly. E.g. park, beach or visit relatives.

Let your child know that you have missed them and are looking forward to hearing what they have been doing with the other parent. Sound enthusiastic to encourage the child.

1. Always be positive about the other parent as children need the support of both parents. Negative talk against the other parent is considered psychologically damaging for the child.

2. If your child reacts negatively when you arrive and doesn't want to go with you, stay calm and ask the child why they are upset.

3. Children can become stressed on access and on occasion can find the alternative arrangements tiring. Children need routine so wherever possible try to make access days the same each week or fortnight. Both parents need to maintain

consistent bedtime and healthy food at appropriate meal times. Allow an hour of relaxation before putting the child to bed.

4. If possible don't pick your child up in a stressed or angry state of mind. Children sense anger or aggression and will react negatively to a tired stressed parent.

5. Whenever possible **don't punish** your child for an **emotional reaction**, this will only make matters worse. Your child did not ask to be in their situation and parents need to show patience with a child "acting out".

6. If your child is naughty then offer "time out" in their room for ten minutes, then assure your child calmly, that their behavior "makes you sad" because you

want the time with your child to be fun. By conversing with your child you will give them assurance that their time with you is special and just for them.

7. Use basic language when explaining your situation to your child, particularly within the family. *E.g.* *"Mummy and Daddy love you very much and we both want you to have fun when you are at both Mummy's house and Daddy's House."*
"Daddy said he wants to hear all about the fun things we do at Mummy's house."

8. Communicate with the other parent as to what activities the child has been doing and choose an activity either different or similar, what ever works best for your child.

9. If you cannot communicate with the other parent introduce a day book so the other parent is aware of what your child has been doing.

10. Children need to know it is alright to have fun when with both parents. They also need to be able to speak about the other parent in a positive manner.

Access for Children

Access arrangements for children is one of the most critical factors involved in a separation and divorce.

Children can have a greater opportunity of security and well being if they have access to both parents. Particularly children who have resided with both parents prior to their separation.

Access is an important part of your child's emotional and physiological development. It is important that the child experiences both parents as one can not make up for the other.

The idea of access is to create as much normality for the child in a time of change and confusion. Equal access is important in child rearing decisions and children spending equal time in both parental homes is the best arrangement.

Access for children can be problematic if there is conflict between the parents. Other issues such as logistics and coordinating the parent's time and schedules can also cause anxiety for all involved.

Children shuttling backwards and forwards with different rules and expectations can cause disagreements that can arise with former spouses.

Communication with your ex-partner in regards to your child's needs will prevent your child from feeling insecure. Insecure children display behavior problems and are more likely to be non compliant.

Access needs to be promoted as a positive experience for your child instead of a negative. Help to encourage your child to look forward to spending time with the other parent.

If children have a healthy relationship with their parents they are more likely to involve you in their lives for years to come.

If the custodial parent supplies warmth and a stable structured environment for the child, than the non-custodial parent can assist the child by providing finical and physiological support to the other parent.

For some couples the hope of shared parenting is abandoned due to the parties needing to remove themselves and create a separate identity. A typical example is women who flee from domestic violence.

In circumstances where a child does not have access to the non-custodial parent, it is important that the caregiver at their discretion explains to the child why they no longer see the other parent. This helps the child to have a clear understanding which promotes awareness and an opportunity to move forward.

The parent tips in "I Have Two Houses" are a guide to making the transition of access as comfortable as possible for all parties concerned.

The story of "I Have Two Houses" gives some awareness of typical reactions that children display when in a separated situation. The story promotes two children who do have equal access arrangements. It gives examples of how the parents devote quality time to the children and cope with a sole parent situation.

While the story is ideal, it is not a fantasy. Parents can make a conscious decision to separate as amicable as possible. There are services such as counselors, family centres and community groups that can assist people who are experiencing difficulties.

Printed in the United States
'"7519LV00002B/77/A